The God of Mercy, The God of the Gospels

PETER McVERRY SJ

VERITAS

Published 2016 by
Veritas Publications
7–8 Lower Abbey Street
Dublin 1
Ireland

publications@veritas.ie
www.veritas.ie

ISBN 978 1 84730 677 7

10 9 8 7 6 5 4 3 2 1

A catalogue record for this book is available from
the British Library.

Designed by Padraig McCormack, Veritas Publications
Front cover incorporates photograph by Sergi Camara
Printed in Ireland by SPRINT-print Ltd, Dublin

Veritas books are printed on paper made from the wood pulp of managed forests. For every tree felled, at least one tree is planted, thereby renewing natural resources.

THE GOD OF MERCY, THE GOD OF THE GOSPELS

CONTENTS

PREFACE

When young people tell me they don't believe in God, I ask them to tell me about the God they don't believe in. I usually end up telling them that I don't believe in that God - a censorious, judgemental God - either; the God I believe in is a God of mercy and compassion, who is tolerant of our weaknesses and forgiving of our offences. This book is an attempt to describe the God that I believe in.

How we understand God determines how we understand what God wants, and therefore it influences our attitudes, priorities and behaviour.

When I was growing up, the God that was presented to me by the Church was a God who was a judge. God was essentially a lawgiver, who had formulated many laws by which we were to live our lives, laws that were affirmed and interpreted by the Church. This God would judge us by our observance of those laws. If we obey them, we will be rewarded with a place in heaven; if we disobey them, we may lose God's friendship forever. God's passion was our observance of those laws.

Every Sunday, then, I went to Mass in order to observe the law of God, to do my duty. One Sunday, I decided I was not going to go to Mass that day, and I didn't. I felt a great weight had been lifted off my shoulders. I had been going to Mass to fulfil an obligation that had been imposed on me. From then on, I went to Mass every Sunday, not because I felt under an *obligation* to go, but because I actively *chose* to go. The constant focus on obeying laws, in order to win God's favour, was oppressive. I was on a fast track to becoming a righteous little Pharisee.

Working with homeless people has made me question this understanding of God. I got close to people whose lives were full of suffering, who had experienced tragic childhoods, the effects of which continued into adulthood. And society often seemed indifferent to their plight, or worse still, judged and condemned them.

The God of the law also appeared irrelevant to their lives. The chief concern of homeless people, like that of refugees fleeing war-torn Syria or impoverished sub-Saharan Africa, is about getting through *this* life, not about the life to come.

The God that I now believe in is one who cares about the suffering and pain of children, a God whose passion is compassion. That God was revealed in the life and death of Jesus. Jesus was the compassion of God to the dispossessed and powerless, he shared meals with those who were rejected by the society of his time, he cured the sick (feeling sorry for him, Jesus touched him and said to him 'be cleansed'. Mk 2:41). Finally, Jesus gave up his own life, so that we might live.

Pope Francis' emphasis on the God of Mercy (mercy, he defined, as 'opening one's heart to wretchedness') is leading us into a different understanding of our relationship with God and has profound implications for the way we live our lives - particularly our spiritual lives. A spirituality that focuses on what I want (getting to Heaven) and on what *I* must do to achieve my goal (obeying God's laws) is replaced by a spirituality that focuses on what *other*s need and what I must do to help them achieve *their* goal.

To grow into the image and likeness of the God of compassion, we have to become the compassion of God to others. The God of compassion is 'good news to the poor' but far more threatening to the lifestyle and securities of those of us who are not poor than the God whose passion is the observance of the law.

INTRODUCTION

Two thousand years ago lived a man who was called Divine, the Son of God and God from God. He was given titles such as Lord, Redeemer, Liberator, Saviour of the World and Prince of Peace. Who was that person? It was the Emperor, Caesar Augustus.

Caesar had conquered the known world; his victories over his enemies had saved his people from the turmoil of constant war and brought peace to the Roman Empire. This new world of peace was attributed to the gods and Caesar was revered throughout the empire as the one sent to bring peace to the world.

In a little corner of that empire, there came into being a small group of people who took the identity of the Emperor of Rome and gave it to a Jewish peasant who had been crucified by the emperor's representative, Pontius Pilate. Clearly this was either a joke, intended to mock Caesar, or it was high treason; but the emperor was scarcely falling around the place with laughter. The early Christians were persecuted, arrested, imprisoned and, on occasion, executed.

Those early Christians clearly understood that their king was not Caesar but the Risen Jesus; that the kingdom which commanded their allegiance was not the Roman Empire but the Kingdom of God. For example, young Christian males refused to serve their time in the Roman army, as commanded by the law of the empire, because the king they followed was Jesus who commanded a radical non-violence. Although they were often arrested and sometimes executed for refusing to obey Caesar, they stood firm in their refusal.

They understood that the Kingdom of God was neither a 'spiritual kingdom' nor merely a kingdom that would manifest itself at the end of time in heaven; it was instead, as Jesus proclaimed, a kingdom in which they were living, here and now, and which radically altered their life on earth.

When Matthew wrote his Gospel, he told the story of the Three Wise Men who came to Jerusalem from the east. They asked:

Where is the infant king of the Jews? We saw his star as it rose and have come to do him homage. (Mt 2:1-2)

Now Herod, Caesar's representative in Galilee, was so enraged at the perceived threat to his authority, he ordered the slaughter of all male children under two years of age. According to Matthew's account, he clearly understood that Jesus would come to undermine him. Matthew makes no attempt to explain that Herod had perhaps misunderstood the Wise Men and that Jesus was really a 'spiritual' leader who posed no challenge to Herod or Caesar. On the contrary, Matthew's story describes how the Three Wise Men fell to their knees to do him homage and offered the gifts traditionally associated with royalty: gold, frankincense and myrrh.

In his Gospel, Luke describes Mary's response to her cousin Elizabeth's affirmation that her son Jesus was the Lord:

> The Almighty ... has used the power of his arm,
> He has routed the arrogant of heart,
> He has pulled down princes from their thrones,
> And raised high the lowly.
> He has filled the starving with good things,
> And sent the rich away empty. (Lk 1:46-55)

Again, Luke makes no attempt to explain that this is to be understood spiritually or metaphorically.

When John – now an old man who had reflected all his life on his years walking with Jesus – was writing his Gospel, he describes Jesus' last few hours in terms of kingship.

Pilate asks him, Are you the King of the Jews? (Jn 18:33) Jesus does not rush in to deny it. Instead he says:

Mine is not a kingdom of this world; if my kingdom were of this world, my men would have fought to prevent my being surrendered to the Jews. (Jn 18:36)

Did Jesus mean that his kingdom was of another world, or did he mean that his kingdom is *in* this world but not *of* it, much as an enclosed monastery of contemplative monks is *in* this world but not *of* it?

What finally forced Pilate to make his mind up was the crowd shouting: If you set him free, you are no friend of Caesar's; anyone who makes himself king is defying Caesar (Jn 19:12).

Pilate then brings Jesus out to the crowd: Here is your King (Jn 19:14).

The crowd replies: We have no King except Caesar (Jn 19:15).

The Gospels present Jesus as a king who poses a threat to the leaders of this world such as Caesar and his representatives, Herod and Pilate. The Kingdom of God, proclaimed by Jesus, was understood to be a kingdom, here and now, in this world; however, the way of life of those in the Kingdom of God was in stark contrast to the way of life lived in all the other kingdoms that were in existence.

Nonetheless, most Christians today still conceive of the Kingdom of God as a heavenly kingdom in another place and another time. Traditional spirituality referred to our time on earth as a pilgrimage: we are on a journey to our true home in heaven and urged to 'judge wisely the things of earth, and love the things of heaven', as one prayer of the Mass relates.

Jesus became incarnate so 'that we may have life, and have it to its fullness'. This is understood, then, to refer to eternal life, and entering eternal life in heaven becomes the focus and objective of our relationship with Jesus.

Such a spirituality is inward-looking, self-centred; our eyes are focused on heaven and what *I* must do to get there. But the spirituality of the Gospels is outward looking, other-centred; our eyes are focused on others and how we can love them.

Perhaps it's all St Matthew's fault; after all, he first called it 'the Kingdom of Heaven'. In deference to the Jewish culture, within which many of the Christians to whom he was writing had grown up, Matthew was reluctant to use the term 'Kingdom of God' out of respect for the awesomeness and holiness of God. So Matthew opted, instead, for the term 'Kingdom of Heaven'. But it would be a mistake to believe that Matthew was referring to a 'spiritual', other-worldly kingdom. No, Matthew was talking about the 'Rule of Heaven', here and now, on earth.

THE MISSION OF JESUS

Everywhere Jesus went, he was followed by large crowds. Five thousand people, not counting women and children, listened to him all day long, even forgetting that they were hungry (cf. Lk 9:10-17). The entire population of every town he visited, we are told, turned out to hear him (cf. Mk 2:2.). The poor man who was paralysed and wanted Jesus to cure him couldn't get near Jesus because of the crowds (cf. Lk 5: 17-26). Large crowds followed him, coming from Galilee, the Decapolis, Jerusalem, Judaea and Transjordan, (Mt 4:25) the Gospel writers tell us.

Who were these people who followed Jesus to hear what he had to say? Few of them were rich; the rich lived in the cities and there is no record of Jesus ever going into the cities – apart from his ill-fated journey to Jerusalem! – to preach. No, Jesus preached in the towns, villages and countryside of Galilee, which is where the ordinary poor lived: people who struggled to feed their families, to pay their taxes – the nobodies of society.

Some of them were destitute, surviving by begging, and despised by the righteous in society. The people who followed Jesus, the people he preached to, were, for the most part, ordinary, poor people. After all, he stated very clearly at the beginning of his ministry that he had come 'to bring the Good News to the Poor'. Who were these 'poor' that Jesus referred to? Were they, as we sometimes hear today, the materially rich but 'spiritually poor'?

The rich and the powerful – the somebodies of his society – amongst whom were to be found the Pharisees, the scribes, the lawyers and the priests, also occasionally listened to what Jesus was saying. But their response was to go away and plot how to get rid of him (cf. Mt 12:14). Clearly, what Jesus was saying was very relevant to the ordinary, poor, sick and outcast people who came to listen to him in their thousands; they were enthused by what he was saying and couldn't get enough of him. Clearly, also, what Jesus was saying was not irrelevant to the rich and powerful because they were infuriated by his words and quickly came to despise him.

So what was Jesus doing and saying that generated such divergent reactions from different social groups?

Today, the message of the Church is supposed to be the continuation of the message of Jesus. Yet, today, so many ordinary people find the message of the Church irrelevant to their lives. Two thousand years ago people flocked to Christ to hear his message; today, they are walking away, uninterested. Has the message changed? That is for you, the reader, to decide.

Who is God?

The fundamental revelation that Jesus came to bring, and which caused such conflict, then as now, was this: 'Who is God?'

A God of the Law

For the religious authorities at the time of Jesus, God was a God of the law. God desires, above all else, that the people of God should obey the law.

The religious authorities had a solid justification for this understanding of God. Their faith told them that God had heard the cries of the people enslaved in Egypt, they had called on God to rescue them from their oppression by the pharaoh. And God heard their cries and sent Moses to lead them out of Egypt. God made a covenant with the people: for his part, God promised to protect them always and to lead them into the promised land; but on their part, they must obey the laws which God was giving them through Moses. These laws instructed them how to live in right relationship with God and with each other: God would be their God and they were to live in justice and peace with each other, according to the law of the covenant.

When Israel was invaded by foreign armies, with the Israelites taken as slaves and scattered to the far corners of the world, the people of God understood that this had happened because they had been unfaithful to the laws of the covenant. Failure to keep the laws, as given by God, meant that the people of God would have torn up the covenant, and God might therefore abandon them. So the focus of all religious instruction was the law, the meaning of the law, the details of the law. God's passion was the observance of the law. If the people failed to keep the law of God, then dire consequences would surely follow.

A God of the law is, necessarily, a God who is a judge, a God who rewards and welcomes those who keep the law but punishes and condemns those who do not keep it. A God of the law is a God who therefore excludes the sinner.

A God of Compassion

Then along came Jesus. Jesus, as he walked the streets of the towns and villages of Galilee, saw the poverty and the suffering of so many people and the rejection by the religious authorities of those who were considered sinners. This state of affairs was justified by the religious leaders who made reference to their God, the God of the law, the God who judges according to the law and who rejects those who fail to keep it.

And Jesus proclaimed a different God, a God of compassion. There is a very important story in Mark's Gospel. Jesus is preaching in the synagogue on the Sabbath. He notices a man with a withered hand. Interestingly, the man does not ask Jesus to cure him; in fact, he does not attract Jesus' attention in any way. It is Jesus who takes the initiative. He says to the man: 'Stand up out here in the middle.' Now Jesus is going to cure the man, but the law forbids him from curing the man for that is to do work, and work was forbidden on the Sabbath. Why does Jesus invite trouble by saying: 'Stand up out here in the middle'?

We are told at the end of the story that the Pharisees met at once and made plans to kill Jesus. If I had been Jesus, I would have taken a different approach: I would have said to the man: 'meet me around the back afterwards, we won't cause any fuss!' The end result would have been the same – the man goes away cured. No, Jesus cures the man in full view of everyone, and breaks the law, because what he is doing is at the heart of the revelation which Jesus came to bring, namely, that God is a God of compassion, and not a God of the law (cf. Mk 3:1-6).

The God of compassion and the God of the law are incompatible. Jesus had no time for legalisms. He was telling the people that in certain circumstances, God actually required them to break the law. This was heresy. Jesus was seen as a threat to the faith of the people of God, and therefore a threat to those whose lifestyle and status in society depended on the faith of the people. Even worse, Jesus, in his preaching, was a threat to the very existence of the people of God, which was conditional on the keeping of the law of the covenant. Caiaphas, the high priest, understood this when he declared:

> It is better that one man should die than the nation perish. (Jn 18:14)

If Jesus rejected a God of the law, how do we explain Jesus saying:

> Do not imagine that I have come to abolish the law or the Prophets. I have come, not to abolish but to complete them. In truth I tell you, till heaven and earth disappear, not one dot, not one little stroke is to disappear from the law until its purpose is achieved. (Mt 5:17-18)

Jesus appears to support the religious authorities' emphasis on keeping the law!

Jesus saw a value in the law: indeed, he considered it very important. Moses had given the law to the people as a way of instructing them how to live in harmony with God and with each other. But it was intended to be an educational tool, not an end in itself.

Anthony de Mello, a Jesuit mystic, tells the story of a person who wanted his friend to see the beautiful sunset. So he points his finger at the sunset and says: 'Look at that beautiful sunset.' Now if the person keeps staring at his finger, they miss the beautiful view! De Mello's comment suggests that the law is like the finger; it is pointing to something beyond itself, namely how to live in right relationship with God and each other.

Saint Paul says the same thing in a different way:

Love can cause no harm to your neighbour, and so love is the fulfilment of the law. (Rm 13:10)

Since the law was intended to show us how to live together as God wants us to, then when we have learnt how to love each other, the law has no further function and we don't have to keep referring back to it, or wondering what it is commanding us to do.

Jesus saw, all around him, in the poverty and exclusion of many of his fellow human beings, the consequences of preaching a God of the law. The poor were unable to keep the law, because they didn't know the law; they didn't know the law because they didn't have the money or education to study it. But because they didn't keep the law, it was understood that they were no friends of God, whose passion was the observance of the law. The God of the law wanted nothing to do with them, and therefore righteous people – the friends of God – wanted nothing to do with them.

The sick, the blind, the lame, the maimed and the lepers were all considered to be under punishment by God for some sin they must have committed. Hence, since they were out of favour with God, their plight deserved no sympathy or response from society.

Similarly, sinners who did not observe the law were to be rejected by society, because they clearly were rejected by the God of the law.

The God of the law is a God who rewards those who keep the law and punishes or excludes those who do not. But Jesus did not preach a God of the law. If Jesus came to give the people new laws, or to reinforce the laws that the religious authorities of his time were preaching, the crowds would not have followed and listened to him. They were, in fact, sick of being oppressed by a multiplicity of laws that they were told they had to obey. No, they listened to Jesus in their thousands all day long because he preached a different God, a God who was good news, a God of compassion.

This conflict between the God of the law and the God of compassion is a fundamental conflict between our Church and spirituality today. We have to admit that our Church has often preached a God of the law. You were identified as a good Catholic by your adherence to a variety of laws and regulations. Your fidelity to the Church's laws and rules was the proof of your fidelity to God. Your relationship to God was defined by your observance of laws – if you do as you are supposed to do, then God is pleased with you and will reward you; if you do not do as you are supposed to do, then God will be angry and punish you. Thus, *our relationship with God is controlled by us*, by our behaviour. But we cannot control our relationship with anyone, still less God!

The dominant image of God, in this spirituality, is that of judge. The Church, like the religious authorities of Jesus' day, excludes those who do not obey the laws which it has declared to be the laws of God. The Church has preached a God who will reward the just with eternal happiness in heaven and punish the sinner with eternal punishment in hell.

Is this why today the message of the Church, which is supposed to be the continuation of the message of Jesus, is seen by so many ordinary people to be irrelevant to their lives? Unlike the thousands of people who enthusiastically followed Jesus when he was alive, today thousands of people, especially the young, are walking away. Are they, like sheep without a shepherd, hungering for a God of compassion and instead being fed a God of the law?

The Prodigal Son

The well-known Parable of the Prodigal Son is the story of two Gods, a God of the law and a God of compassion. The younger son, who knows he is a sinner, is entirely dependent on the father being a father of mercy. He prostrates himself before his father's compassion. The elder brother does not want his father to be compassionate. He wants his father to be a God of the law, a God who rewards the just (him) and punishes the wicked (his younger brother). But to his dismay, the father treats the sinful brother even more affectionately than he treated the 'just' brother and rejoices at his unexpected return! The just brother, who has always done everything within his power to please his father, resents this.

The father pleads with the elder brother, making it very clear that, although he loves him very much and is very grateful for all that he has done for him, he (God) is not a God of the law but a God of compassion who does not condemn sinners but instead reaches out and welcomes them.

Then Jesus said, 'There was a man who had two sons. The younger of them said to his father, "Father, give me the share of the property that will belong to me." So he divided his property between them. A few days later the younger son gathered all he had and travelled to a distant country, and there he squandered his property in dissolute living. When he had spent everything, a severe famine took place throughout that country, and he began to be in need. So he went and hired himself out to one of the citizens of that country, who sent him to his fields to feed the pigs. He would gladly have filled himself with the pods that the pigs were eating; and no one gave him anything. But when he came to himself he said, "How many of my father's hired hands have bread enough and to spare, but here I am dying of hunger! I will get up and go to my father, and I will say to him, 'Father, I have sinned against heaven and before you; I am no longer worthy to be called your son; treat me like one of your hired hands.'" So he set off and went to his father. But while he was still far off, his father saw him and was filled with compassion; he ran and put his arms around him and kissed him. Then the son said to him, "Father, I have sinned against heaven and before you; I am no longer worthy to be called your son." But the father said to his slaves, "Quickly, bring out a robe – the best one – and put it on him; put a ring on his finger and sandals on his feet. And get the fatted calf and kill it, and let us eat and celebrate; for this son of mine was dead and is alive again; he was lost and is found!" And they began to celebrate.

'Now his elder son was in the field; and when he came and approached the house, he heard music and dancing. He called one of the slaves and asked what was going on. He replied, "Your brother has come, and your father has killed the fatted calf, because he has got him back safe and sound." Then he became angry and refused to go in. His father came out and began to plead with him. But he answered his father, "Listen! For all these years I have been working like a slave for you, and I have never disobeyed your command; yet you have never given me even a young goat so that I might celebrate with my friends. But when this son of yours came back, who has devoured your property with prostitutes, you killed the fatted calf for him!" Then the father said to him, "Son, you are always with me, and all that is mine is yours. But we had to celebrate and rejoice, because this brother of yours was dead and has come to life; he was lost and has been found."' (Lk 15:11-32)

The elder brother's reservations will resonate with all of us who are doing our best to live good lives according to our understanding of the will of God. Compared to those whom we consider to be leading selfish and self-centred lives, we can easily come to believe that God 'owes' us. If God does not express disapproval of, or condemn in some fashion, those whose lives are sinful, then what is the point in the rest of us trying to live good lives with all the sacrifices and effort that requires? If sinners are going to get the same – or an even warmer! – welcome from God, why should we bother? So thought the elder brother, and all of us who have the elder brother inside us.

Only those who appreciate that they are sinners can truly welcome a God-whose-passion-is-compassion. The God-whose-passion-is-observance-of-the-law offers only condemnation to sinners. Sinners cannot rely on their good works to save them, for they have none; they depend on God's compassion. To them, the God that Jesus revealed was, indeed, good news, for it opened the Kingdom of God to them. That kingdom had been firmly closed to them by the God who rewards the good and punishes the wicked, the God-whose-passion-is-observance-of-the-law.

Those who believe themselves to be righteous, however, prefer to believe in a God-whose-passion-is-observance-of-the-law. They have the most to gain from such a God, who, they believe, will give them their just reward in the next life. The God of compassion appears to undervalue all their efforts to live a good life, as these may count for nothing in the next life.

Hence, Jesus was welcomed enthusiastically by many who believed themselves to be rejected by God, but was rejected by many who believed themselves to be righteous. The God that Jesus revealed was good news to sinners, but bad news for the righteous, who instead of receiving an exclusive reward from God for their efforts, saw sinners getting the same welcome from God as themselves.

How do you preach a God of the law? Why, you get scholars to study the law and examine all the different situations in which the law might apply, and then you tell people what they are supposed to do. You can preach the God of the law from an ivory tower, surrounded by your important books.

But you cannot preach the God of compassion in that way. To reveal the God of compassion, you have to *be* the compassion of God. You cannot merely preach the God of compassion from a pulpit. You can only preach the God of compassion if you are immersed in the poverty and suffering, the homelessness and hopelessness of people around you. It is that real poverty and suffering, homelessness and hopelessness that the God of compassion addresses. And so to understand the revelation of Jesus – that God is compassion – we cannot disconnect Jesus from the society into which he was born, and in which he lived and died. We have to look at the suffering of the people of that time, and the economic, social and political conditions which caused that suffering, just as we have to do today if we are to preach a God of compassion. Perhaps we have disconnected Jesus from the real, concrete suffering of the people of his time, because it challenges us, even threatens us.

THE KINGDOM OF HEROD

So what was that society like? Jesus was born into the Kingdom of Caesar. Now Caesar had appointed Herod as Tetrarch (or king) of Galilee to keep control of that territory, which Herod did with utter ruthlessness. Herod had no reservations in slaughtering all the male children under the age of two, one of whom, he had been told, would become King of Israel and was therefore a threat to his authority.

A few years before Jesus was born, Herod had burnt forty Jews to death for trying to lead a protest against Roman occupation. When Jesus was three or four years old, two thousand Jews were crucified in the city of Sepphoris – only about five miles from Nazareth where Jesus lived – and its inhabitants exiled into slavery, as a reprisal for an attempted revolt against Caesar. Life had little value in Caesar's kingdom; it was entirely dependent on the whim of Caesar or his representatives.

Jesus came to a people who were cruelly oppressed by Caesar and his empire.

He also came to a people of whom the vast majority lived at a subsistence level. They lived from day to day, never sure where tomorrow's food would come from. When Jesus asked them to pray: Give us this day our daily bread, the sentiment was a literal rather than a figurative one, as it is today for those millions living on the edge of starvation. For most of us, however, it is a prayer whose meaning is purely metaphorical.

Many also lived on the edge of destitution: those with infirmities, the blind, the lame, the deaf, the dumb, the lepers. They had no quality of life, instead theirs was a very precarious existence and they were forced to beg just to stay alive.

Others were rejected, unwanted and marginalised: those who were considered to be sinners, with no regard for the law. They were despised and ostracised. A small minority, perhaps 7 to 8 per cent, were ostentatiously wealthy, with no concern for the poor and the hungry around them. They included the royal court, the priests and religious aristocracy who became wealthy through the buying and selling of sacrificial offerings in the Temple. They also included the rich landowners, many of them Herod's friends, who had accumulated farms by the policy of confiscating land from small landowners, often on the pretext that they were unable to pay the exorbitant tax that Herod demanded of them. But Herod didn't need much in the way of pretext, he had absolute power to do whatever he wanted, and there was no court of appeal.

This was God's chosen people, oppressed both from without and from within, struggling to survive and to maintain any sense of their own dignity: rejected by their fellow human beings and told that they had also been rejected by God. This was not what God had in mind when he liberated the people from Egypt and led them into the promised land. This was not a people over whom God could possibly want to reign.

THE KINGDOM OF GOD

And Jesus came proclaiming a new kingdom, the Kingdom of God, over whom God would happily reign. And Jesus told people stories about this new Kingdom of God that was coming. Jesus talked about the rich man who feasted sumptuously every day and was dressed in the finest linen (Lk 16:19-31) and who couldn't even be bothered to gather up the crumbs that fell from his table to give them to the poor man at his gate. The people Jesus conversed with knew exactly, some from their own experience, what he was talking about. And when Jesus went on to say that the rich man would be cast down to Hades and Lazarus would be welcomed into the Kingdom of God, you can imagine them looking at one another and nodding their heads in approval. Their own religious leaders were telling them that there would be no place for them in God's kingdom because they had been rejected by the God of the law, and here was Jesus telling them about a God, a God of compassion, who would welcome them into God's kingdom. When Jesus declared that in the Kingdom of God: 'The first shall be last and the last shall be first', they thought of the rich and respectable who considered themselves better than the poor and the infirm, and they were overjoyed. No wonder they could listen to him all day. This was indeed good news to the poor and rejected.

And when Jesus talked about the rich landowner (cf. Lk 12:13-21) who, following a massive harvest, said to himself: 'What I am to do? I know, I will tear down my barns and build bigger ones', without any consideration for those around him who were hungry, the people Jesus was talking to knew exactly what part of town these guys lived in. And when Jesus said that God is going to require his soul tonight, you can imagine them smiling with approval. This was indeed a God they would want to believe in.

And when Jesus talked about the large landowner (cf. Mt 21:33-46) who sent his servants to collect his share of the produce from his tenants (often demanding as much as half of the produce for himself) and the tenants beat the servants and sent them off, they must have applauded loudly. Now the Gospel writers have made this story into an allegory, where the large landowner is God, the servants are the prophets and the son, whom they put to death, is Jesus. However, almost certainly the original story that Jesus must have told many times was the story of the exploitation of the tenants by the large landowners.

These were not 'made-up' stories; Jesus was telling it as it was. And he was telling them that, in the Kingdom of God that was coming, their lives were going to be very different. And when Jesus talked about the labourers (cf. Mt 20:1-16) who waited in the market square all day hoping to get a few hours work, they knew exactly what Jesus was talking about: some of them, no doubt, had 'been there, done that'. And when Jesus said that even those who were given work at the eleventh hour also received the same wage, one denarius – enough to feed their family for the day – they were astounded; they never heard of any rich vineyard owner doing such a thing. A rich landowner who actually cared whether his workers had enough food or not! And when Jesus tells them that the rich vineyard owner is like God, they are filled with wonder – could God really be a God who cares, who cares about them and whether their families will get fed? They want to hear more about this wonderful God.

But Jesus didn't just *tell* people about the God of compassion. When Jesus healed the blind and the lame and the lepers, who were told by their own religious leaders that they were cursed by God, in the very act of being healed they *experienced* the God of compassion that Jesus revealed. This was a God beyond all their expectations. It is no wonder those who were cured went off and told everyone what Jesus had done, even when Jesus had instructed them to tell nobody (cf. Mk 1:44-45). How could you not go and tell everyone about this God of compassion and love?

And when Jesus ate with sinners (cf. Mt 9:9-13), who were told by their own religious leaders that they were forsaken by the God of the law, in their table fellowship with Jesus they *experienced* the unconditional forgiveness of the God of compassion. This was not just 'Good News' – this was extraordinary news, beyond all their expectations. And when Jesus reached out, in friendship, to the unwanted and marginalised, who were told by their own religious leaders that God had rejected them, they *experienced* God's acceptance of them. This is what they had not even dared to hope for, and now it was becoming a reality for them.

And Jesus tells them the story of the Pharisee (cf. Lk 18:9-14), who reminded God of all his merits and good works, and the publican, who had no good deeds to present to God. When Jesus announces that the publican, not the Pharisee, went home more justified before God, they were given hope and encouragement which they had never experienced before.

And when the rich young man (cf. Lk 18:18-23) wants to follow Jesus, he is told that he must first share his wealth with the poor. When he is unable to do so, he is sent away, sad. You can hear some heckler in the audience shouting up: 'Good for you, Jesus. That guy doesn't care about us. He cannot be part of our kingdom.'

To understand the revelation of Jesus, perhaps you have to be angry. Love and anger are two sides of the same coin:

you cannot love someone who is suffering unnecessarily without being angry at their suffering. Jesus was angry, not by the people's failure to keep the law, but by the poverty and marginalisation of people which was imposed upon them by the law.

Jesus was angry by the unnecessary suffering of the people he met as he walked the roads of Galilee and entered the towns and villages there, a suffering which the law did nothing to relieve.

Jesus was angry when he cast the sellers out of the temple courtyard. (Mt 21:12-13)

Jesus was angry when he called the Pharisees hypocrites, who lay heavy burdens on peoples shoulders (burdens of guilt imposed by the God of the law), but will not lift a finger to help them carry them (Mt 23:4).

Jesus was angry when he called the Pharisees imposters, who take advantage of widows and rob them of their homes (Mt 23:15).

Jesus was angry when he called the teachers of the law whitewashed tombs, which look fine on the outside, but are full of dead men's bones and rotten stuff on the inside (Mt 23:27).

Jesus is telling those who came to listen about a kingdom where those on the margins of society will be welcomed, respected, and valued instead of being rejected where people will reach out to the poor, and share what they have, so that their needs will be met, instead of being ignored and despised by those who had the resources to meet their needs. In this new kingdom, people will live in a totally different way to the way they now had to live. People will live by totally different values to those of the society around them. In this new kingdom, their king will be, not the brutal Herod or the warmongering Caesar, but God, a God of compassion, a God who cares.

The God who liberated the people from their oppression in pharaoh's kingdom is now coming, indeed has already come, to liberate the people once again, this time from their suffering in Caesar's kingdom, which oppressed them with the collusion of the priests and religious aristocracy.

So they wanted to know: where was this new kingdom to be found? And what did they have to do to enter this kingdom?

A Community of Radical Solidarity

The early Church, after the death and Resurrection of Jesus, understood that they were to continue the mission of Jesus, to reveal the God of compassion by *being* the compassion of God to each other and to the world. The way of life of this Christian community caused such astonishment to the pagans that their spontaneous response was: 'See how they love one another.' Their leader and king, the one they followed and the model for their life together, was the risen Jesus, Son of God, who continued to be present amongst them. In this community, the Kingdom of God that Jesus had promised was close at hand, was now present in our world.

I read the Gospels now, not as instructions to me as to how I should live my life according to the moral laws of God which Jesus revealed, but as instructions to the early Christian community – and therefore to us, as the Christian community in our time – as to how we are to live together in order to be the Kingdom of God on earth.

And so I read the story of the feeding of the five thousand who had spent the whole day listening to Jesus. In the evening, the disciples had to go up to Jesus and say: 'Jesus, would you ever shut up! The people are hungry. Send them off to the towns and villages around, so that they can get something to eat.' The whole point of the story, for the early Christian community, lies in Jesus' answer to the disciples:

No, you give them something to eat yourselves. (Lk 9:13)

The Christian community understood that this was an instruction from Jesus to them. They were to ensure that they reached out to those among them who were in need and not leave their needs unmet.

The Kingdom of God is where God lives, where God is to be found. In the famous Last Judgement scene, we read:

I was hungry and you gave me to eat, I was thirsty and you gave me to drink, I was naked and you clothed me, I was in hospital and you visited me, I was in prison and you came to see me. Welcome into the Kingdom prepared for you from the foundation of the world. (cf. Mt 25:31-46) (Mt 25:34-36)

Perhaps Matthew is not talking about judgement at all. Perhaps Matthew is describing a community where God is present. A community that reaches out to feed the hungry, to give water to the thirsty, to clothe the naked; in other words, to meet the needs of all. A community that expresses the compassion of God in its life together is a community where you will find present the God of compassion. Welcome into the Kingdom.

But a community which fails to reach out to meet the needs of all is a community where God, the God of compassion, is absent:

> I was hungry and you did not give me to eat, I was thirsty and you did not give me to drink, I was naked and you did not clothe me, I was in hospital and in prison and you did not visit me ... Depart from me. (Mt 25:42-43)

The early Christians understood that, to enter the Christian community – the Kingdom of God – a person took on the responsibility of *being* the compassion of God *to* one another. Hence, they were to live together in radical solidarity with each other, loving each other with a love that was willing to share everything for the sake of those in need. Just as Jesus had given up everything, including what was most precious to him – his own life – for our sake, so they, as followers of Jesus, were to be prepared to give up everything, even what may be most precious to them, for the sake of their brothers and sisters. They understood that all they had were gifts, given to them by God, not so that they could have a good life and enjoy themselves (like the guy in the kingdom of Caesar who built bigger barns to store his harvest), but so that they (now living in the Kingdom of God) could use them for the benefit of others. They were, therefore, to share their resources, their time, their talents, their skills for the sake of those who needed them. And so the rich young man, a good young man, a young man who had kept all the commandments from his youth, whom, we are told, Jesus looked on … and loved (Mk 10:21), nevertheless, he could not become a follower of Jesus, could not be admitted to the early Christian community, because his unwillingness to share what he had for the sake of those in need was a contradiction to everything that Jesus lived and preached, an obstacle to revealing a God of compassion by being the compassion of God.

A COMMUNITY OF
RADICAL INCLUSIVENESS

One of the characteristics of Jesus' life that was remembered and passed down from generation to generation of Christians in those early communities was the fact that Jesus shared table fellowship with sinners:

Jesus ate with tax collectors and sinners. (Mt 9:9-13)

This caused Jesus endless difficulties. Righteous people asked: 'How could this man be from God, when he associates with the enemies of God, those who do not keep the law?' The God of the law cannot tolerate the actions of the God of compassion.

How would the early Christian community understand these words when they heard them read at the Sunday Eucharist? Jesus they knew to be God; God eating would bring to mind the Kingdom of God in heaven, which was often portrayed as a meal at which God presides.

Master, who shall be at the feast in the Kingdom of God? (Lk 14:15)

And who will be present at that meal? Why, those who were excluded and unwanted here on earth in the kingdom of Caesar. And so they reasoned, if they will be welcomed amongst God's guests in the Kingdom of God in heaven, then they should also be welcomed in their community, the Kingdom of God on earth.

The early community understood that this radical inclusiveness, revealed by the actions of Jesus, was normative for their community and life together. In their community, no one was to be ignored, rejected or marginalised. Everyone has the same dignity of being a child of God and that dignity was to be recognised and affirmed by the way in which the Christian community reached out to them and accepted them.

A COMMUNITY OF
RADICAL NON-VIOLENCE

When Jesus was arrested, one of his followers, traditionally understood to be Peter, drew his sword and cut off the ear of the high priest's servant. Jesus told him:

> Put your sword back, for all who draw the sword will die by the sword. Or do you not think that I can appeal to my Father, who would promptly send more than twelve legions of angels to my defence. (Mt 26:51-53)

Matthew includes this little story, which is otherwise quite irrelevant to the arrest of Jesus, to illustrate that the way of Jesus is a way of non-violence.

The Passover Feast – Celebrating Freedom

The last week of Jesus' life was spent in Jerusalem. He went up to Jerusalem for the most important feast of the Jewish year, the Passover. During this week, tens of thousands of Jews made the pilgrimage up to the temple in Jerusalem, the place where God dwelt. It was a dangerous time for the political authorities – the Passover feast celebrated the liberation of

Israel from their foreign oppressors in Egypt. There were among them some who wished to see the liberation of Israel from their Roman oppressors and were prepared to use violence to achieve it. Hence, during this week, the Romans fortified their garrison in Jerusalem with a large number of soldiers drafted in from outlying barracks.

On the Sunday before the feast – which, as Christians, we celebrate as Palm Sunday – the Roman governor, Pontius Pilate, rode into Jerusalem, seated on his magnificent horse, along with a large garrison of cavalry and foot soldiers, thousands of soldiers with weapons and shields and spears, gold eagles mounted on poles, to the sound of the beating of drums. Crowds of people would have come out to witness such rich pageantry. This procession of the Roman governor and his soldiers was not just the symbol of a political system that created and maintained poverty, enormous inequality and oppression, it was the very means by which this system maintained itself.

At the same time of the same day, Palm Sunday, Jesus also entered Jerusalem, from the other side of the city, seated on a donkey. This was not a coincidence: this procession was planned in advance by Jesus and carefully thought out:

> When they had come near Jerusalem and had reached Bethphage, at the Mount of Olives, Jesus sent two

disciples, saying to them, 'Go into the village ahead of you, and immediately you will find a donkey tied, and a colt with her; untie them and bring them to me. If anyone says anything to you, just say this, "The Lord needs them". And he will send them immediately.'

This took place to fulfil what had been spoken through the prophet, saying, 'Tell the daughter of Zion, Look, your king is coming to you, humble, and mounted on a donkey, and on a colt, the foal of a donkey.' The disciples went and did as Jesus had directed them; they brought the donkey and the colt, and put their cloaks on them, and he sat on them.

A very large crowd spread their cloaks on the road, and others cut branches from the trees and spread them on the road. The crowds that went ahead of him and that followed were shouting, 'Hosanna to the Son of David! Blessed is the one who comes in the name of the Lord! Hosanna in the highest heaven!' When he entered Jerusalem, the whole city was in turmoil, asking, 'Who is this?' The crowds were saying, 'This is the prophet Jesus from Nazareth in Galilee'. (Mt 21:1-11)

This was a symbolic act on Jesus' part, intended to contrast with the procession of Pontius Pilate. Matthew tells us the meaning of Jesus' entry into Jerusalem in this way:

This took place to fulfil what had been spoken through the prophet, saying, 'Tell the daughter of Zion, Look, your king is coming to you, humble, and mounted on a donkey, and on a colt, the foal of a donkey.' (Mt 25:4-5)

The full text of the prophet that Matthew quotes is:

Rejoice greatly, O daughter Zion! Shout aloud, O daughter Jerusalem! Lo, your king comes to you; triumphant and victorious is he, humble and riding on a donkey, on a colt, the foal of a donkey.

He will cut off the chariot from Ephraim and the war horse from Jerusalem; and the battle bow shall be cut off, and he shall command peace to the nations; his dominion shall be from sea to sea, and from the River to the ends of the earth. (Zech 9:9-10)

The reign of Jesus was to be a reign of peace which would banish chariots, war horses and swords; this reign would be from sea to sea, to the ends of the earth. It would abolish the reign of Caesar and every other reign where injustice, oppression and war existed. Jesus intended his procession – which today we would call a 'counter-demonstration' – to contrast the two reigns, the reign of God or the reign of Caesar, two very different visions of life on earth.

A Community of
Radical Quality

In this community, not only were economic relationships to be transformed, but social and political relationships too:

> At that time the disciples came to Jesus and asked, 'Who is the greatest in the kingdom of heaven?' He called a child, whom he put among them, and said, 'Truly I tell you, unless you change and become like children, you will never enter the kingdom of heaven. Whoever becomes humble like this child is the greatest in the kingdom of heaven.' (Mt 18:1-5)

The children in the passage above are often understood to be welcomed by Jesus because of their innocence. However, it is far more likely that Jesus was referring to their lack of esteem in society. Children in that society had little value, as they had no achievements to point to as evidence of their importance.

Those who think they are more important than others will be disillusioned! Those who think they are of lesser value will be overjoyed:

Look, there are those now last who will be first and
those now first who will be last. (Lk 13:30)

In this community, all relationships are based on equality.
There is to be no differentiation of status in this community:
everyone is equal, except the leader of this community, the
Risen Jesus:

But you are not to be called rabbi, for you have one
Teacher, and you are all students. And call no one your
father on earth, for you have one Father – the one in
heaven. Nor are you to be called instructors, for you
have one instructor, the Messiah. The greatest among
you will be your servant. All who exalt themselves will
be humbled, and all who humble themselves will be
exalted. (Mt 23:8-12)

The community established by Jesus was to be a
community of brothers and sisters, free of all domination.
Jesus is Lord and there is no other; Jesus is teacher and
there is no other; Jesus is priest, mediator between God and
human beings, and there is no other.

This community is the reign of God in history – God is
king of this community and there is no other. God identified
himself with Jesus and so God's reign is the reign of Jesus.

The equality that characterises the reign of God occurs in the incarnation itself. God came to the people of God, not by identifying with a religious or priestly leader, not by identifying with someone in authority, but by identifying with a crucified victim of religious and political oppression. This crucified victim, the least in the kingdom of Caesar, is leader and king, the first in the Kingdom of God.

LEADERSHIP WITHIN THE COMMUNITY

Jesus warned the early community against replicating, within the new community, the relationships of power that existed in the wider society:

> But Jesus called them to him and said, 'You know that the rulers of the Gentiles lord it over them, and their great ones are tyrants over them. It will not be so among you; but whoever wishes to be great among you must be our servant, and whoever wishes to be first among you must be your slave; just as the Son of Man came not to be served but to serve, and to give his life a ransom for many.' (Mt 20:25-28)

The request of the mother of Zebedee to give her sons a position of power in the Kingdom of God suggests that she failed completely to understand the nature of the kingdom that Jesus was inaugurating:

> Then the mother of the sons of Zebedee came to him with her sons, and kneeling before him, she asked a favour of him. And he said to her, 'What do you want?'

She said to him, 'Declare that these two sons of mine will sit, one at your right hand and one at your left, in your kingdom.' But Jesus answered, 'You do not know what you are asking. Are you able to drink the cup that I am about to drink?' They said to him, 'We are able.' He said to them, 'You will indeed drink my cup, but to sit at my right hand and at my left, this is not mine to grant, but it is for those for whom it has been prepared by my Father.'

When the ten heard it, they were angry with the two brothers. But Jesus called them to him and said, 'You know that the rulers of the Gentiles lord it over them, and their great ones are tyrants over them. It will not be so among you; but whoever wishes to be great among you must be your servant, and whoever wishes to be first among you must be your slave; just as the Son of Man came not to be served but to serve, and to give his life as a ransom for many.' (Mt 20:20-28)

Jesus himself showed the apostles what leadership meant in the Kingdom of God:

They were at supper … Jesus got up from the table, removed his outer garments, and taking a towel, wrapped it round his waist; he then poured water into a basin and began to wash the disciples' feet and to wipe them with the towel he was wearing … When he had washed their feet and put on his outer garments again, he went back to the table. 'Do you understand,' he said, 'what I have done to you? You call me Master and Lord, and rightly, so I am. If I, then, the Lord and Master, have washed your feet, you must wash each other's feet. I have given you an example so that you may copy what I have done to you.' (Jn 13:2-15)

John, already an old man when he wrote his Gospel, had pondered all his life on this scene, which occurred at the beginning of Jesus' last meal with his disciples. It had clearly made an indelible impression on him. He records it in his Gospel because he considers it normative for the Christian community to which he belonged. Leadership and power within the community was only for service, not for personal benefit or status.

A Kingdom like No Other

When Jesus is arrested and brought before Pilate, Pilate asks him: 'Are you the King of the Jews?' Jesus answers:

> Mine is not a kingdom of this world. If my kingdom were of this world, my men would have fought to prevent my being surrendered to the Jews. (Jn 18:33-36)

This saying of Jesus is often understood to mean that Jesus' kingdom is to be found in the next world, not in this one. But the Gospels are very clear that Jesus understood that the Kingdom of God, which he was inaugurating, was coming into this world. It was not a spiritual or otherworldly kingdom. It was in this world, but not of this world – the values by which those in the Kingdom of God were to live were utterly different from the values by which those in any other kingdom in this world lived. The kingdoms of this world were kingdoms of greed, inequality, where abuse of power was the norm, kingdoms which came into existence through violence, and were maintained by violence. The Kingdom of God was, by contrast, a kingdom of nonviolence, equality, caring and sharing, reaching out to the unwanted, where power was the power to serve, not to oppress. This new community was a kingdom over which God, in the person of Jesus, reigns.

The Kingdom of God was to be in this world, a light for all to see. This community of radically different economic, social and political relationships was to be a model for the world.

> You are the salt of the earth; but if salt has lost its taste, how can its saltiness be restored? It is no longer good for anything, but is thrown out and trampled underfoot.

> You are the light of the world. A city built on a hill cannot be hid. No one after lighting a lamp puts it under the bushel basket, but on the lamp-stand, and it gives light to all in the house. In the same way, let your light shine before others, so that they may see your good works and give glory to your Father in heaven. (Mt 5:14-16)

This community had a missionary mandate:

> Go therefore and make disciples of all nations, baptising them in the name of the Father and of the Son and of the Holy Spirit, and teaching them to obey everything that I have commanded you. And remember, I am with you always, to the end of the age. (Mt 28:19-20)

This new community, then, represents, in history, what God desires for all humanity in the face of poverty, oppression and violence – a community which lives together in solidarity and equality, and so in justice and peace, over whom God can reign. This community is 100 per cent religious and 100 per cent political.

The hope and salvation of all humanity are to be found in this community.

This Community is Not for All

This community lives in a radically different way from all other communities. Its members are those who have listened to the call of the king who invites them to transform this world through a radical solidarity with all others, to follow him who gave his life for them by giving their own lives, and everything they have and are, for their brothers and sisters.

Before one joins this community, then, it is necessary to sit down and think long and hard as to whether one can live this way of life:

> For which of you, intending to build a tower, does not first sit down and estimate the cost, to see whether he has enough to complete it? (Lk 14:28-33)

In other words, before entering this community, sit down and decide if you can really live this way. Can you live in radical solidarity with everyone else in this community, including the poor, thereby ensuring that the needs of everyone are met? Can you live in a relationship of equality, respect and dignity with everyone else in this community, including those rejected by society?

If so, then you are welcome; if not, you may be a wonderful, hard-working, upright, morally just person – and God will love you for it – but a place in this community is not for you.

Don't join this community and then regret it in a few months' time!

Otherwise, if he laid the foundation and then found himself unable to finish the work, anyone who saw it would start making fun of him and saying, 'Here is someone who started to build and was unable to finish'. Or again, what king, marching to war against another king, would not sit down first and consider whether with ten thousand men he could stand up to the other who was advancing against him with twenty thousand? If not, then while the other king was still a long way off, he would send envoys to sue for peace.

So in the same way, none of you can be my disciple without giving up all that he owns. (Lk 14:29-33)

The Sacraments

The sacraments have a central place in the life of this community. But how we understand the sacraments depends on how we understand who God is and why Jesus became incarnate.

If God is a God of the law, who sent Jesus to instruct us how, as individuals, we are to live our lives according to the laws that God has laid down, and thereby earn a place in heaven, then the sacraments become occasions of grace for us as individuals and a means to salvation. People then celebrate the sacraments because God wants them to do so.

However, if God is a God of compassion, who sent Jesus to proclaim the Kingdom of God, to show us how to live together as a community over which God reigns, then the sacraments become significant events in the life of that community.

All communities celebrate special moments in the life of their members. They have celebrations when new arrivals join the community; they celebrate events that they consider significant for the community; they celebrate the appointment or election of leaders to the community.

So too the Christian community, a community of people who lives together in a radically new way – with radically different values to the way of life and values of the societies within which they live – celebrates those moments of special importance. These celebrations are called sacraments.

- **Sacrament of Baptism** is the celebration of the community at the entry into their midst of a new member.

- **Sacrament of Confirmation** is the celebration of the community when one of their children reaches adulthood.

- **Sacrament of Marriage** is the celebration of the community at the commitment in love of two members for each other.

- **Sacrament of the Sick** is the prayer of the community for healing or a happy death of one of their community.

- **Sacrament of Holy Orders** is the anointing of one of the community to be a leader of that community.

- **Sacrament of the Eucharist** is the community celebrating the self-sacrificing love of Jesus revealed in his death, his continuing presence to them as the Risen Lord, and re-affirming their commitment to love one another as Jesus loved them.

- **Sacrament of Penance** is the request to the community for forgiveness from someone who has offended another within the community.

Divorced from community, the sacraments have become, for many Christians, social occasions, events dictated by social convention, rituals to be performed, frequently boring and irrelevant to their 'real' lives, but they may, nevertheless, participate out of a sense of duty and obedience. For example, the Eucharist may become 'a Sunday duty'. The Sacrament of Penance has been abandoned by many who see it as unnecessary and irrelevant in its present form.

The Sacrament of Penance

Our understanding of sin and reconciliation depends on our understanding of God.

If God is a God of the law, then sin is a transgression of God's law, an offence against God, and requires us to be reconciled to God in the Sacrament of Penance. The priest is understood to be the representative of God. Absolution from the priest is the guarantee of God's forgiveness.

However, if God is a God of compassion, who calls us to live in love and build a community of peace and justice, then sin is understood to be that which causes suffering to another, either deliberately or through wilful negligence. In any community there will be arguments, rows and hurtful remarks or actions which cause offence and need healing. Every community requires some process for restoring relationships that have been frayed or broken, and reconciling people who have hurt others and been hurt by others. Such a process of reconciliation is an integral part of the life of any community, as, without it, the community will fall apart.

The Sacrament of Penance was that mechanism for the Christian community. It was a structured way in which people could come to the community and confess that they had hurt others, and the members of the community would accept their repentance and restore relationships that had been broken. Hence the Sacrament of Penance was an essential part of the structure of the early Christian community.

Reconciliation is then primarily reconciliation of people with each other and the priest in the Sacrament of Penance is primarily a representative of the community. However, since those who have been hurt are God's children, then reconciliation with God is also part of the Sacrament of Penance (often referred to as the Sacrament and Reconciliation). But the reconciliation with God occurs *in the very act* of reconciliation between people.

The community founded by Jesus had only one rule: 'love one another as I have loved you.' Forgiveness is the highest expression of love. As God's love and forgiveness is infinite and unconditional, so the love and forgiveness of the members of the community of Jesus was to be exceptional.

Hence in the Gospels, Jesus emphasises, again and again, the need for reconciliation and forgiveness within the community:

> Then Peter came and said to him, 'Lord, if another member of the Church sins against me, how often should I forgive? As many as seven times?' Jesus said to him, 'Not seven times, but, I tell you, seventy-seven times'. (Mt 18:21-35)

Seven was the number that signified perfection. Hence Peter was really asking: 'Must my forgiveness be perfect?' Jesus replies: 'not only perfect, but way, way beyond perfect.'

Structural Sin

Imagine a road with a bad bend. There are many road accidents at this bend, many people are injured. If I am concerned by the suffering of those who are injured, there are two possible ways in which I can respond:

1. I can raise money to provide a mobile first-aid clinic where the bend is located. Then, when an accident occurs, there are medical personnel on hand to help the injured. This undoubtedly is a response, in compassion, to the suffering of others.

2. However, I might decide to lobby the local authority to get them to straighten the road. If successful, there will be no more accidents at this part of the road, and I have succeeded in preventing a lot of suffering. This political response is also an act of compassion, motivated by the desire to prevent unnecessary suffering to others. This political response is, indeed, much more effective than setting up a mobile clinic.

If sin is that which causes unnecessary suffering to another, we have to acknowledge that, in our complex world today, the unnecessary suffering that many people experience is caused not so much by the actions of one individual against another, rather by the way our societies are organised. Many theologians now talk about 'social sin' or 'structural sin'. If sin is understood, not as the transgression of a law (the God of the law), but as the cause of suffering to another (the God of compassion), then structural sin is the suffering that *a system* inflicts on others. It is their suffering that makes the sin in the structures real and visible.

Structural sin has been defined by Bernard Connor OP, who lived in apartheid South Africa, as 'the abiding deficiencies or wounds in the way society is structured'. Sinful structures emerge as a result of a cumulative series of personal sins, sometimes going back generations, implicating not only those who made the policy decisions, but also those who supported and worked for the system, and those who remained silent and did nothing to change it.

Thus the generals in the military regime in Burma, for instance, who seized power in 1962 in a military coup, were responsible for the suffering, over many decades, of the people of Burma, but so too were their successors who annulled the democratic elections which they lost decisively in 1990; so too were those who benefited financially by supporting the regime, army officers who kept them in power and all those citizens who failed to oppose them. All share responsibility for that suffering.

Closer to home, politicians who fail to legislate to ensure that Travellers do not have to live on the roadside, local officials who fail to plan for suitable halting sites and accommodation, those who oppose Travellers being accommodated in their neighbourhoods, and all of us who do not protest at the conditions in which they continue to live, all share responsibility for their plight.

It can be difficult for us to accept that structures can be sinful. In our traditional understanding of sin as personal, it is clear who has sinned and therefore who should repent and make amends. If I hit you on the head and rob you, it is very clear who is the culprit and who is the victim. A sinful act is traditionally linked to a particular individual, and the consequences of that sinful act or omission is evident in the harm that it causes to others. However, the blame for the suffering caused by sinful structures cannot be laid at the feet of any specific individuals. It seems as if everyone and no one is guilty. It is hard to know who should repent!

It is even more difficult for us to accept responsibility for the suffering caused by sinful structures. The connection between our actions and their harmful effects can be very complex. Purchasing a tracksuit in a reputable Dublin shop may be linked to the exploitation of children working in sweatshop conditions in a faraway country. There is no intention to harm anyone. The link is via a complex, global structure. As we do not directly experience the consequences of our actions on others thousands of miles away, we may feel no obligation to accept responsibility for deconstructing the sinful structures that are unconsciously maintained by our actions.

Furthermore, the complexity of the structures creates a sense of powerlessness to do anything effective about them, even if we wanted to. We can feel imprisoned within the structures, unable either to change them or escape from them. We feel powerless before the might of the system.

The Role of Ideology

But there is another, even greater, difficulty in acknowledging our responsibility for structural sin: our own lack of awareness. Economic, social and political structures are legitimised and normalised by the images and concepts that shape the way we see reality. The ideological structure of society can blind people to the immorality of their involvement in the structures.

For example, today we find it unimaginable that a society could tolerate slavery. But for hundreds of years, societies, God-fearing, Church-going people not only tolerated slavery but justified it. Even St Paul had no difficulties with slavery. The Church in the US, in the eighteenth and nineteenth centuries, had no problem with the concept of owning slaves. The structure became embedded in the psyche, and those who benefitted from it failed to see its inherent sinfulness.

This should make us aware that today we are living in structures that are unjust, but because they have become so much a part of the fabric of our lives we fail to challenge them. For example, I may regret that people are homeless and living on the streets, but can believe that this is merely the inevitable consequence of economic development – some people, unfortunately, just get left behind. Some people are unemployed, but I may believe that this is just the way capitalism works – indeed, I might argue, quite rightly, that capitalism *requires* a small pool of unemployed people just to function properly. This is just the way things are, and there is nothing anyone can do, or need do, about it. So we have internalised the unjust system. How often have we heard people say: 'Most poor people on benefits are too lazy to work', or 'they have it too good on welfare' or 'many homeless people *choose* to live on the streets'. We internalise, and therefore normalise and legitimise the sinful structure that is in front of our eyes.

We also have to acknowledge that there may be sinful structures within our churches that are causing pain and suffering to some, or marginalising others, but that, again, we have internalised and legitimised. We have become convinced that such structures are 'normal' and 'the way things are'. And so we are blinded to the pain they cause, and do not recognise their sinfulness.

Thus, as a person internalises the system as constructed by society, the sinful structure becomes *part and parcel of the person themselves*. We become totally unaware of the sinfulness inherent in the way we live and we can be convinced that we are upright citizens and faithful followers of the Gospel.

Have you eyes and do not see [*the suffering of others*], ears and do not hear [*their cries*]? (Mk 8:18)

Thus, if we believe that suffering is inevitable and merely a regrettable by-product of the status quo, then, of course, we can avoid any sense of guilt and our comfort zones are not disturbed. Sin only arises when a situation that causes pain or suffering to others both can, and should, be changed – but isn't.

And so, too, the victims of the structures. Sinful structures may also become part and parcel of the mindset of the victims themselves. They too can become convinced that this is just the way things are – unfortunate but inevitable. They too can come to be convinced that they are not the victims of an unjust set of structures that should be overcome, but just the unfortunate victims of a system that is inevitable and therefore unchangeable, or, worse still, that the way things are is 'God's will'. They, too, have internalised the structures, which makes it very difficult for them to challenge and overcome them.

Response to Social Sin

Believing in a God of compassion, who passionately wants the suffering of God's children to end, compels us to seek to change the structures of our societies and of our world that keep people in poverty and on the margins.

Faced with sinful structures, apathy or neutrality is not possible; our apathy becomes, rather, an option *for* the structures. As Albert Nolan OP, a priest who lived in apartheid South Africa, wrote:

> Any preaching of the Gospel that tries to remain neutral with regard to issues that deeply affect the lives of people, like the issue of the rich and the poor, is in fact taking sides. It is taking sides with the status quo, even if that is not its intention, because its neutrality prevents change. (Lectures on the Theology of Liberation)

Sometimes the response to structural sin is to seek to replace the leaders in a society, or to dismantle structures that are identifiable with a particular group in society. The Marxist concept of class struggle would be an example of such a response to perceived unjust structures. But this is to ignore the fact that the structures have become embedded, hidden in the consciousness both of the beneficiaries of the structures and of its victims, and structural reforms, *on their own*, leave that consciousness intact. Structural reforms must be accompanied by conscientisation, *including our own.*

Social sin is only acknowledged when it is being overcome. While I may not be personally responsible for the creation of a sinful structure, I have a responsibility for overcoming it. The acceptance of that responsibility is a radical moment of grace for a person.

Prophets are those who reveal the will of God. Prophets live on the dangerous interface between politics and religion. They are persecuted by righteous people who want to sleep well in their beds. But prophets themselves rarely die in bed of old age! They speak up, act decisively and pay dearly. Proclaiming the God of compassion had political implications for the society of Jesus' time, and personal implications for him; and so it will for us.

The community of God is called to be prophetic, to reveal the God of compassion to the world by the struggle to make our world a more just place. It seeks, in the name of God, to challenge and change those sinful structures that are causing suffering to others, both close and far away. It must commit itself to social justice. It will, therefore, invite persecution from those who seek to maintain the structures.

THE EUCHARIST

The Eucharist is at the centre of the life of the community of God and of each of its members. How we understand the Eucharist depends on our understanding of God, our spirituality.

If God is a God of the law, who sent Jesus to tell us how to live our lives according to the law of God, then we may understand the Eucharist as primarily a source of the grace which is necessary for our eternal salvation. We go to Mass to 'do our duty'.

What is happening at the Eucharist is, then, something other-worldly. When we go into the church, we leave this world and all its temporal cares and problems behind. The Eucharist is primarily a time of worship, of prayer. It is about the affirmation of Jesus as Lord and God, an affirmation that leads us into the presence of God. In the Eucharist, then, where we acknowledge that Jesus is the Son of God, the grace of the sacrament is given to us to guide us on our path to heaven.

This understanding of the Eucharist has been shaped primarily by Arius and Constantine, both of whom lived about 300AD. This understanding – though of course perfectly valid and theologically correct – no longer, it seems to me, meets the needs of many Christians today.

Arius denied that Jesus was truly divine. A lot of people came to follow his teaching. So the Church went into overdrive to counter this heresy. Acknowledging Jesus as God, which was taken for granted by the early Church, now became *the* defining characteristic of Christian identity. The celebration of the Eucharist became predominantly an act of worship of God in Jesus. The impact of that continues today in our own eucharistic celebrations: benediction and adoration of the Blessed Sacrament became a very important part of the spiritual life of Catholics, attendance at Sunday Mass became the hallmark of a committed Catholic and evidence of their belonging to the Church. After the consecration, the priest raises the host and the chalice to allow the congregation to worship God, now present there. Receiving Holy Communion was only legitimate for those who were in the state of grace, and therefore worthy to receive the Body and Blood of Christ. Reverence for the divinity present in the bread and wine required the faithful to fast from midnight before receiving the Body and Blood of Christ.

Since the Eucharist had become primarily an act of worship of God in Jesus, how it was celebrated was strictly controlled by Rome to preserve the sacredness of the occasion. In churches around the world, in Africa, Europe, North America, Latin America, Australia and Asia, exactly the same ritual was enacted, the priest wearing exactly the same kind of vestments, with his back to the people, using a language that people did not understand, the chalice had to be lined with gold to defined specifications, the wine had to have a specific alcoholic content, the priest extended and joined his hands at exactly the same places in the rubric, in every little village around the globe. The celebration of the sacrament required total control to avoid the possibility of any abuse and to preserve the sacredness of the occasion.

The Second Vatican Council came along and introduced some relatively minor variations: the Mass was now said in the vernacular; the priest actually faced the people while saying Mass; Communion could be received in the hand; you only had to fast for one hour before receiving Communion. These were changes that were fiercely resisted by many, both priests and laity, who believed that they diminished the reverence due to the Divine Presence in the Eucharist. Some of us can recall priests who refused to give Communion in the hand, and there are some today, priests and laity alike, who wish to go back to the sacred character of the Latin Mass, which they believe has been lost in present-day liturgies.

This understanding of the Eucharist, as adoration of God in Jesus made present in the Eucharist, was compounded by the adoption of Christianity as the official religion of the Roman Empire by the Emperor Constantine. Churches were built in cities and towns throughout the empire, and the Eucharist was now celebrated no longer in secrecy in the homes of Christians for fear of persecution, but in the public space. As befitting the majesty of God, churches became more ornate, magnificent cathedrals were built as monuments to the glory of God, and the Eucharist was celebrated with incense and ever more elaborate music. Gregorian chant became the music form considered the most sacred, and therefore the most suitable, for the celebration of the divinity revealed in Jesus.

Outside the walls of the churches, wars were being fought, revolutions were being waged, feudal society gave way to the industrial revolution, kings were being toppled. But inside the walls of the churches, the same Eucharist was celebrated in exactly the same way, oblivious to what was going on outside. The Eucharist, understood to be an act of worship, of adoration, was for people a means of personal sanctification, sanctity understood as 'otherworldly'. The focus is firmly on heaven, on saving our souls. Through our worship of Jesus as Son of God in the Eucharist, grace is poured out on us. The Eucharist is understood as an indispensable requirement for salvation.

This understanding of the Eucharist is based on the words of Jesus at the Last Supper, when Jesus said 'This is my body, this is my blood … do this in memory of me.' And so the priest takes the bread and the wine and they are transformed into the Body and Blood of Jesus.

However, at the Last Supper, Jesus did not say: This is my Body, this is my Blood and invite the disciples to worship him. Jesus actually said: This is my Body, which will be given up for you and This is my Blood, which will be poured out for you, and he invited the disciples to follow him.

In a spirituality that is focused on others and their needs, the Eucharist then becomes, first of all, a time to remember: to remember, in thanksgiving, how this community, to which we have committed ourselves, began, namely through the total self-sacrifice of its founder and leader, the Risen Jesus, and to recall, once again, the core value of self-sacrificing love by which the community is called to live.

And, second, in Communion, in receiving the Body and Blood of Jesus, we unite ourselves with Jesus. Receiving Communion then becomes an act of radical commitment: we commit ourselves to following Jesus, to be united with him, in his total self-sacrificing love.

The Eucharist, then, is at the centre of the life of this community to which we belong. This community of radical solidarity, inclusiveness and non-violence is not a left-wing social experiment. It differs from this by the fact that its leader is the Risen Jesus. We give our lives not for some ideology but for a person.

But if we, and this Christian community, are not living this life of self-sacrificing love, then going to Eucharist becomes meaningless. Perhaps our young people today find no relevance in the Eucharist we celebrate, because it has lost its meaning.

If the Eucharist is a sacrament through which I, as an individual, receive grace which will assist me in reaching my goal, which is heaven, then isn't it wonderful that the millionaire and the pauper can sit side by side at Mass, week after week, worship the same God and receive the same grace, regardless of their different circumstances and status? The God of the law makes no distinction between rich and poor, both are offered the same law, the same grace and the same reward.

But if the Eucharist is a commitment to living a life of self-sacrificing love for the sake of my neighbour, then there is a total contradiction in the millionaire and the pauper sitting side by side at Mass, week after week.

We go to Mass then, not to do our duty, but to commit ourselves to leaving Mass to do our duty – namely, to reveal the God of compassion by being the compassion of God.

CONCLUSION

A small child, Jesus of Nazareth, born two thousand years ago, was then, and is now, the revelation of God's hope for our world. In this child, the human and the divine have become one, forever inseparable. Other religions might tell us that we encounter God in sacred places, in temples, places of worship, but we Christians believe that, because of this child Jesus, we encounter God in other human beings.

> In truth I tell you, in so far as you did this to one of the least of these brothers of mine, you did it to me. (Mt 25:40)

And while other religions might tell us to worship God with sacred actions, with sacrifices and prayers, we Christians, because of this child Jesus, worship God by loving God in each other, by caring about and reaching out to our fellow human beings.

> I give you a new commandment, love one another; you must love one another as I have loved you. (Jn 13:34)

Jesus had a dream. His dream was God's dream. He dreamt that all people would live together as one family,

God's family. In a family of four children, the parents do not give three of the children a nice steak for their dinner, and give the fourth child bread and jam; no, everyone shares what little they may have. Yet that is what the family of God does to one billion people on our planet who live on the edge of destitution. Each of those one billion people is God's beloved child. No parent wants their child to go hungry every night. God does not want God's children to live like this.

In a family of four children, the parents do not give three of the children a nice warm bed to sleep in and tell the fourth child to sleep outside on the porch. This is not how God wants God's family to live. No, the children share whatever rooms they have in the house. Yet that is what the family of God does to homeless people in every city of our world. No parent wants their child to sleep on the street. And God does not want God's children to sleep on the street.

Jesus dreamt of a world where no one would be hungry and have nothing to eat, where no one would be thirsty and have nothing to drink, where no one would be naked and have nothing to wear, where no one would be sick and have no one to visit them, where no one would be in prison and rejected by their community (cf. Mt 25). He was put to death by the religious and political leaders who did not want to see his dream become reality. He was put to death by those who did not want to share their wealth with the poor, by those who wanted to hold on to power for their own self-interests, by those who objected to the tax collectors, the prostitutes and the sinners, refused to associate with them and pushed them to the margins of society.

Jesus dreamt that all people would love each other, care for each other, share with each other, respect each other.

What unites us as Christians is that we share this dream of Jesus. To declare ourselves as followers of Jesus is to announce to the world that we have committed our lives to building this dream that Jesus passed on to us. This passion for building a world of justice and peace, in which all people live together as God's people, is the distinguishing characteristic by which Jesus wanted his followers to be identified:

> By this shall all know that you are my disciples, by your love for one another. (Jn 13:35)

To transform the world from where it is today to where God would like it to be tomorrow requires a revolution. That revolution is the community of Christians, which Jesus called the Kingdom of God. We, that community, have a lot of soul-searching, a lot of hard thinking to do. Does the life of this community reflect the vision of God for our world? Or would Jesus find the same inequalities, injustice and marginalisation in this community as he found two thousand years ago? Does the life of the Christian community, and the relationships within it, challenge the values and practices of the wider society in which it exists, in a way that brings persecution and rejection from that society? Or does the Christian community sit comfortably in society, indistinguishable from it? Have we betrayed the trust that God has placed in us, have we rationalised away the Gospel to suit our own interests and comforts? Are we prepared for the radical conversion that would transform our relationships with each other, particularly with the poor and marginalised?

We are called to listen long and hard to the Gospel, to the call of the king who invites us to transform this world through a radical solidarity with all others, to follow him who gave his life for us by giving our own lives, and everything we have and are, for our brothers and sisters.

We are called to listen to a call to a radical personal conversion that would revolutionise our world. This self-sacrificing love for others has such radical consequences for the way we live together, that it threatens many in our society today, just as it did two thousand years ago. This self-sacrificing love is incompatible with the inequalities of wealth and power that exist in our society and in our world. In a community that loves one another, there should be no one poor, unless all are poor; there should be no one homeless, no one lonely, no one sick and alone, no one in prison who has been abandoned or written off; there should be no one rejected or marginalised, if we truly loved one another as God has loved us. God's dream, of a world that loves with the radical unselfish love of God, is good news to some but bad news to others.

Now, as then, there are many who do not want this dream to become reality. Then, Herod sought to destroy that dream by slaughtering the children; the powerful sought to destroy that dream by executing Jesus. Now, there are many who are attached to wealth and power, who feel threatened by God's message of caring and sharing, of solidarity with the poor and the needy, of using power, not for self-serving purposes, but for serving others, who will resist – often with violence – God's call to build a community of love. There are those who abuse their power for their own self-serving interests, while people wait in poverty and powerlessness for the changes that could transform their lives but which those in power resist. There are those who will not reach out to the homeless, the drug user, the prisoner, those in social housing, but will reject them, want nothing to do with them, and push them to the margins of their society. Those who commit themselves to building God's dream will face opposition, ridicule and rejection, as Jesus once did. Today there are more civilised ways of crucifying people: we will be labelled 'idealists', or 'Marxists', be told to 'live in the real world' and not 'in dreamland'. But we Christians do live in dream land, we live in God's dream.

But the crucifixion, then as now, isn't just the inevitable *consequence* of dreaming of a new world that challenged those who wanted their old world to remain. The crucifixion *is* the road, the only road, that can make this dream come true. The crucifixion of Jesus was the total self-giving of Jesus for our sake, the sacrifice of everything that was important to Jesus, even his own life, so that we might have life. Today, as then, God's dream can only be realised through the same total self-giving of those who dream that dream, through the same radically selfless love that is willing to sacrifice ourselves for the sake of others. A just world cannot be built through economic growth alone; it can only be built by the self-sacrifice of those whose passion is compassion, who are willing to care and share what they have and who they are, who are prepared to 'lose their life' so that others may live. All religions call on their followers to love one another. But we Christians are the ones who have heard the call 'to love one another *as I have loved you*'. Jesus gave his life for our sake; to follow him is to accept his invitation to give our lives for the sake of our brothers and sisters.

Those who are poor, who are sick, in hospital, living alone, those in prison, or homeless, those who are unemployed, offer us, in their need, a great gift, in fact the greatest gift of all. They invite us to open our hearts to include them in our love. If we expand our hearts to include them in our love, we become more loving persons, and so we become more fully human, and therefore more fully divine. Nobody can offer us a greater gift.

If Jesus Christ today is to offer hope to those who are struggling, who live on the edge, who feel unwanted, that hope is you and I. If we do not care and share, if we do not reach out, then there is no hope, and we will have destroyed, yet again, God's dream for our world. A community where everyone's needs are met through the caring and sharing of each person in the community, where everyone feels loved, valued and respected, would surely be the Kingdom of God on earth.